Oceans and Seas

Stephen Savage

KINGFISHER

NEW YORK

KINGFISHER
LONDON & NEW YORK

Copyright © Kingfisher 2010
Published in the United States by Kingfisher,
175 Fifth Avenue, New York, NY 10010
Kingfisher is an imprint of Macmillan Children's Books, London.
All rights reserved.

Illustrations by Peter Bull Art Studio

First published in hardback in 2010 by Kingfisher
This edition published in 2012 by Kingfisher

Distributed in the U.S. and Canada by Macmillan,
175 Fifth Avenue, New York, NY 10010

Library of Congress Cataloging-in-Publication data
has been applied for.

ISBN: 978-0-7534-6866-1

Kingfisher books are available for special promotions and
premiums. For details contact: Special Markets Department,
Macmillan, 175 Fifth Avenue, New York, NY 10010.

For more information, please visit
www.kingfisherpublications.com

Printed in China
1 3 5 7 9 8 6 4 2
1TR/0512/UTD/WKT/140MA/C

Picture credits

**The Publisher would like to thank the following
for permission to reproduce their material
(t = top, b = bottom, c = center, l = left, r = right):**
Page 4l Photolibrary/Sakis Papadopoulos; 5tl Science Photo
Library (SPL)/Planetary Visions; 5tr Nature Picture Library (NPL)/
Georgette Douwma; 5bl Corbis/Karl Weatherly; 5br Alamy/
blickwinkel; 7 Photolibrary/Iain Sarjeant; 8c Photolibrary/
Marevision; 8bl Frank Lane Picture Agency (FLPA)/Yva
Momatiuk & John Eastcott; 9tl Alamy/Premier; 8tr Photolibrary/
Marevision; 8bc FLPA/FotoNatura/FN/Minden; 9br FLPA/Roger
Tidman; 10 Corbis/Stephen Frink/Science Faction; 12cl
Photolibrary/David B. Fleetham; 12b NPL/Georgette Douwma;
12–13t Photolibrary/James Watt; 13tr Photolibrary/Roberto
Rinaldi; 13cl Shutterstock; 13cr Corbis/Stuart Westmorland
Science Faction; 13b NPL/Constantinos Petrinos; 14 Corbis/
Norbert Wu/Science Faction; 16c Photolibrary/Reinhard
Dirscherl; 16b Photolibrary/Reinhard Dirscherl; 17tr Corbis/
Jonathan Blair; 17cr Corbis/Adam Woolfitt; 17bl Photolibrary/
David B. Fleetham; 17br National Geographic Society/Emory
Kristof; 18 Alamy/Photo Agency EYE; 20tl Corbis/Tim Davis;
20cr Getty Images/Flickr; 21ct Alamy/WaterFrame; 2cr Corbis/
Hal Beral; 21bl Corbis/Paul Souders; 21br FLPA/D P Wilson;
23 NPL/Mark Carwardine; 24tl Photolibrary/Koji Kitagawa;
24cr FLPA/Norbert Wu; 24b NPL/Steven Kazlowski; 25tl NPL/
Jim Watt; 25cr Corbis/Rick Price; 25b Photolibrary/Corbis;
26 NPL/David Shale; 28tl Image Quest Marine/Carlos Villoch;
29tl SPL/RIA Novosti; 29tr Photolibrary/Paulo De Oliveira;
29cr Image Quest Marine/Peter Batson; 29bl Corbis/Ralph
White; 29br Monterey Bay Aquarium Research Institute,
California; 30cl Shutterstock/Gregor Kervina;
30cr Shutterstock/Juriah Mosin; 30bl Shutterstock/Kuzma;
31tr Shutterstock/Irina Yun; 31cl Shutterstock/Ocean Image
Photography; 31b Shutterstock/Gary Yim

Contents

More to explore

On some of the pages in this book, you will find colored buttons with symbols on them. There are four different colors, and each belongs to a different topic. Choose a topic, follow its colored buttons through the book, and you'll make some interesting discoveries of your own.

For example, on page 6, you'll find a blue button, like this, next to some children investigating rock pools. The blue buttons are about people exploring.

Page 23

People exploring

There is a page number in the button. Turn to that page (page 23) to find a blue button next to something else that people follow and explore. Follow all of the steps through the book, and at the end you'll find out how the steps are linked and discover even more information about this topic.

Animals

Conservation   **Science**

The other topics in this book are animals, conservation, and science. Follow the steps and see what you can discover!

Oceans and seas

The oceans form the largest habitat on Earth, stretching from shallow coastal seas to wide open oceans and down to the dark depths. Seas are part of the oceans. In fact, all of the oceans are linked together, forming one huge body of water.

This is the Atlantic Ocean near Lagos, Portugal.

The shallow coastal waters are safe for wading and swimming.

A wave, formed out in the ocean, is breaking on the beach.

Coasts are the places where land and sea or ocean meet. They range from beautiful sandy beaches to rugged rocky cliffs. The water there rises and falls twice a day, and these movements are called tides.

Most sandy beaches are made up of tiny pieces of rocks and seashells.

This is the Atlantic Ocean.

This is a sea—the Mediterranean Sea.

Earth is sometimes known as the "blue planet" because almost two-thirds of its surface is salt water in the form of oceans and seas. They control our climate and weather and are an important part of the water cycle.

The oceans are precious. Thousands of animal species depend on them, and humans do, too. The ocean habitat is easily damaged, so it is important that we look after the oceans and use natural resources more wisely.

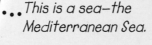

fishing boat

People love to live near the ocean and enjoy water sports such as surfing, sailing, and windsurfing.

At the seashore

The seashore is the place where the land meets the sea. It can be a sandy or pebbly beach, a mud flat or a steep cliff. Much of the seashore is uncovered only at low tide, when rock pools appear and we can take a peek at sea life.

Page 10

Page 23

1 shore crab

2 children playing and looking for sea life

3 blenny (a fish)

4 mussels

This is bladder wrack seaweed. Its air pockets help it float on the surface of the sea.

What is this?

Page 15

As the tide goes out and the sea level drops, many sea creatures stay where they are. Some are stuck on to the rocks and cannot move, while others shelter among the rocks that become rock pools. Crabs and shrimp search for scraps of food, while starfish glide along, feeding on mussels.

5 shrimp

6 periwinkle, a type of sea snail

7 starfish feeding on mussels

8 turnstones looking for food

Between the tides

The lives of seashore animals depend on the rise and fall of the tide. At low tide, animals take shelter among rocks or hide within their sandy burrows. Wading birds come down to the sand to feed.

A scorpion fish hides at the bottom of a rock pool.

seal trapped in a net

Litter floating in the sea can injure and kill wildlife. Animals can swallow litter and choke on it. Many whales, seals, turtles, and sea birds become entangled in old fishing nets and drown.

Scorpion fish are often found in rock pools but are difficult to see because their body pattern matches the surroundings. They lie in wait, ready to gulp down any shrimp or small fish that comes too close.

This unlucky shrimp is about to become a meal for the scorpion fish!

A cockle has feeding tubes that it uses to eat tiny creatures.

Hermit crabs do not grow their own shells like other crabs do. Instead, they live inside empty seashells to protect the soft parts of their body. As a crab grows, it must find a bigger shell.

Wading birds feed on sandy shores and muddy estuaries at low tide. Each species has a special type of beak suitable for reaching the shellfish and worms that live at different depths beneath the sand.

The oystercatcher can eat worms and open mussel shells.

The ringed plover has a short beak to catch animals just beneath the surface.

A coral landscape

A coral reef is like a colorful underwater city, built by millions of tiny animals called coral polyps. Hundreds of different types of fish and invertebrates (animals without backbones) find food and shelter in the coral reef, too, and it is bursting with color and life.

What is this?

Page 19

1 brightly colored butterfly fish

2 blacktip reef shark cruising the reef

3 giant clam, which can reach 4 ft. (1.3m) long

? This is a close-up view of the knobby coral skeleton of staghorn coral.

Page 26

Coral polyps are the quiet heart of this lively scene. These tiny animals grow stony skeletons that protect their soft bodies. They live on the surface of their skeletons and catch food with stinging tentacles. All of the coral skeletons make a huge reef, where hundreds of fish swim and feed. Larger animals, such as sharks, may visit, too.

(4) staghorn coral, a common reef-building coral

(5) brain coral that looks like a human brain

(6) clown fish swimming safely within the tentacles of an anemone

Life on the reef

The reef is home to a surprising variety of animals. It provides them with food and shelter. Some reef fish hunt among the corals, while others find food in more unusual ways.

manta ray

cleaner wrasse

Manta rays swim gracefully through the water by flapping their large winglike fins. They are the largest of all the rays and can measure 16 feet (five meters) from wingtip to wingtip. These fish are harmless to humans and feed on plankton.

Cleaner wrasses set up cleaning stations where they gobble up flealike creatures that live on other fish. A wrasse performs a dance to attract a "customer," who may even allow the wrasse to clean inside its mouth.

This colorful fish has a mouth like a parrot's beak.

Parrotfish use their strong beaklike teeth to feed on algae and coral polyps. Any coral skeleton that they swallow is ground up by teeth in their throat. Some sand around coral reefs is actually parrotfish droppings.

These large fleshy horns guide water and plankton into the ray's mouth

Lionfish are brightly colored as a warning: they're poisonous!

This coral is white, or bleached, because the algae that lived in its polyps have died.

Healthy coral reefs are brightly colored and full of life. Special algae living inside the coral polyps provide extra food needed by the corals to build their stony skeletons.

Algae (the green spots) live in the coral.

Corals are damaged when seas get hotter because of global warming. Higher temperatures kill the algae. Without the extra food from the algae, the coral polyps die and other marine life disappears.

What is this?

1 longfin bannerfish

2 underwater camera

3 People dive in pairs for safety.

Page 27

Exploring a wreck

Lying hidden on the world's seabeds are many shipwrecks—the sad remains of journeys that ended in disaster. Diving to explore these shipwrecks is a fascinating chance to discover hidden history or experience marine life up close.

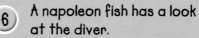

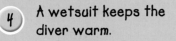

Page 22

Divers explore a shipwreck and discover that this human-made object has become part of the ocean world, home to many different animals. They find sponges and corals growing on the deck and watch schools of brightly colored fish dart to shelter inside the ship. They also meet moray eel and barracuda, lurking and looking for a meal.

This is a close-up view of a sea urchin's spines, which protect it from predators.

Stories under the sea

Every shipwreck has a story to tell. Many sank in storms, while others were the result of sea battles. The objects found onboard and the ships themselves provide valuable information about life in the past as well as clues to how the ships sank.

The mast of this ship can still be seen, and there may be plenty for archaeologists to investigate inside the wreck.

soft coral growing on the wreck

A marine archaeologist
is a historian who studies human history underwater—shipwrecks! This one is carefully exploring a shipwreck full of glass bottles and jars that sank in the 11th century (1000s).

A shipwreck
in a tropical ocean may become a miniature coral reef. These wrecks make exciting sites for divers to explore as almost every surface is covered in marine life.

These objects will be displayed in a museum.

coins from the British shipwreck the Mary Rose (1545)

Bluestripe snapper cruise around a wreck.

The *Titanic* sank in 1912, and 1,517 people died. In 1985, the explorer Robert Ballard discovered this famous shipwreck at about 12,500 feet (3,800 meters) deep.

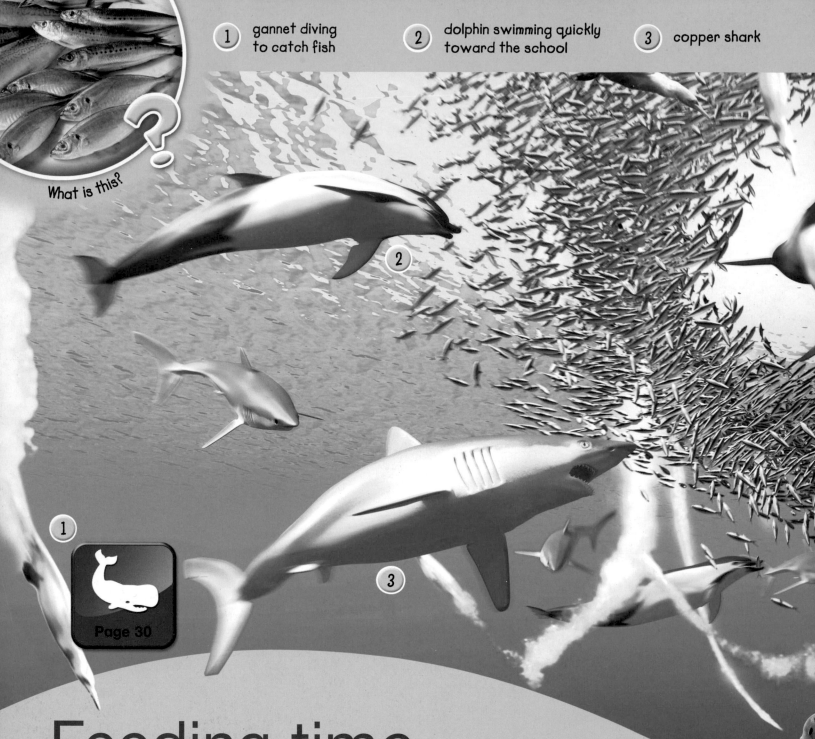

What is this?

1 gannet diving to catch fish

2 dolphin swimming quickly toward the school

3 copper shark

Page 30

Feeding time

In the open ocean, there is nowhere to hide, and many small fish live in big groups called schools. A school is an easy target for attack but gives each fish a better chance of survival. Sharks, dolphins, seals, and diving birds attack all at the same time.

5

4

Page 23

During the summer, enormous schools of sardines travel along Africa's eastern coast, feeding on plankton. These sardines are swimming as a swirling mass of silvery fish called a bait ball. Many predators are attracted to this bait ball. They avoid each other and instead concentrate on catching the fish.

6

This is a close-up view of some sardines—there may be hundreds of thousands in a bait ball.

Oceans full of food

Ocean animals have developed many different ways to find and eat a meal. There are fast and fearsome hunters and slow, gentle plant eaters. There are masters of camouflage that can creep up unseen and whales that scoop up a huge mouthful of water.

Dolphins use their powerful tail to swim fast, and their flippers for steering.

Green sea turtles feed on sea grasses and algae.

Dolphins are meat eaters.

Green turtles dive for up to five minutes to feed.

Dolphins often work together to catch their prey—for example, when they chase a sardine bait ball. They swim fast and catch fish and squids using their sharp pointed teeth. They swallow their food whole.

A cuttlefish is a meat eater.

Leafy sea dragons are camouflaged to look like floating seaweed. They drift through the seaweed hunting small fish and shrimp.

A cuttlefish has suckers on its eight arms to hold on to the food it catches.

A cuttlefish catches prey by shooting out two long tentacles. It has a strong beak that can even bite through a crab's tough shell. When attacked, a cuttlefish can squirt out ink as a defense.

Sea dragons eat tiny plankton.

Many ocean animals feed on tiny plant and animal plankton.

A humpback whale eats tiny plankton.

Huge **humpback whales** feed on tiny plankton, too. Instead of teeth, they have bristly baleen plates, which they use to sieve tiny food from the water.

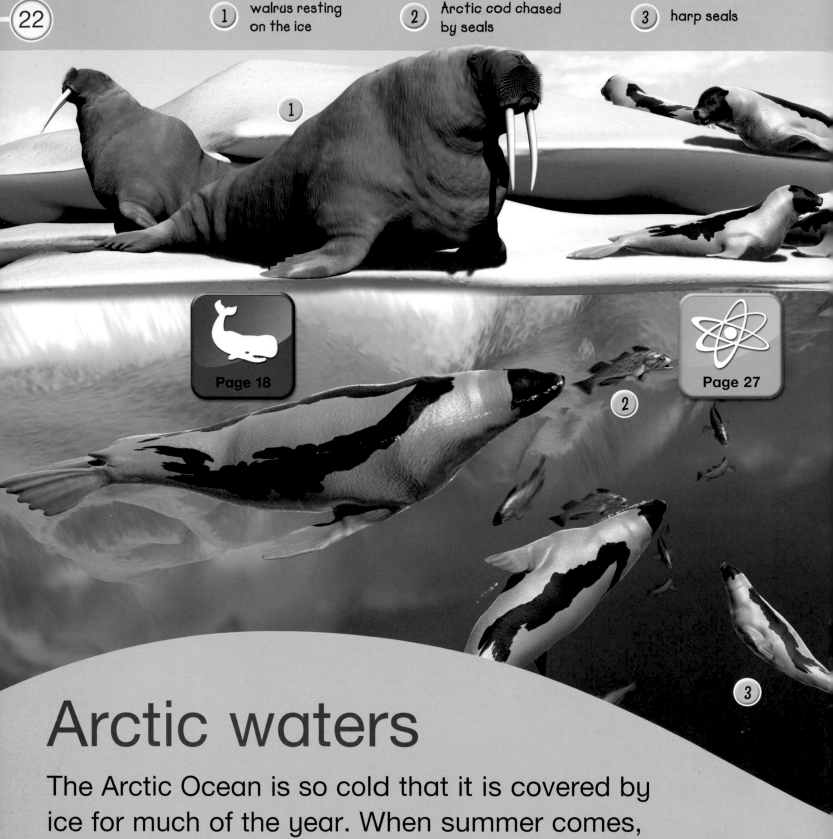

1

Page 18

Page 27

2

3

Arctic waters

The Arctic Ocean is so cold that it is covered by ice for much of the year. When summer comes, the sea ice begins to melt, and the Arctic bursts into life. Many birds and mammals, both large and small, travel north to these rich feeding grounds.

④ Arctic terns visit the Arctic each summer.

⑤ Beluga whale calves are born gray.

⑥ humpback whale

Page 30

Page 14

What is this?

A pod, or group, of beluga whales glides through the icy water. These white whales spend all year in the Arctic. The seals and walrus are here all year long, too. They feed underwater but rest on land. All of these mammals have a thick layer of fatty blubber under their skin to keep them warm.

This is a close-up view of a walrus's whiskers. Like all mammals, the walrus has hair.

Polar seas

In the summer, the Arctic has sunlight for 24 hours a day. Sunlight allows large amounts of plankton to grow, providing food for the animals that live there and attracting summer visitors. When it is summer in the Antarctic, the same happens there.

Seals are born on land. Newborn harp seal pups have a white fur coat. This snowy camouflage helps protect them against predators such as polar bears.

The lion's mane jellyfish is the longest animal, with tentacles 100 ft. (30m) long.

Polar bears spend much of their time on the sea ice hunting seals. They can also swim for hours at a time using their large, powerful front paws as paddles.

This humpback whale calf was born in the winter in the warm, calm seas near Hawaii.

This large sea spider lives on the Antarctic seabed.

Adult humpback whales eat more than 2,200 pounds (1,000 kilograms) of tiny animals a day.

The Antarctic is home to thousands of penguins. These birds dive into the water to catch shrimp and fish.

Adélie penguins live on the Antarctic ice.

Humpback whales visit the Arctic each summer to feed. They build up fat, which they then live off for about eight months while they travel back to warmer seas for the winter.

Penguins cannot fly but are excellent swimmers.

Voyage to the deep

Far beneath the surface of the ocean, where the sunlight cannot reach, there lurk many strange and unusual animals. It is much too far down for a human to swim, but people can explore these depths from manned submersibles.

Page 22

What is this?

 gulper eel with a huge mouth for scooping

 fang fish with big, sharp fangs (teeth)

3 deep-sea squids

This is a close-up photo of an anglerfish's lure. The lure attracts fish into its mouth.

27

A submersible travels into a world of fearsome-looking animals. They are attracted by the submersible's searchlights. Scary-looking fish with needle-sharp teeth and a gulper eel with a giant mouth swim by. Strange creatures that make their own light in the darkness drift past.

Page 30

Page 30

4 Deep-sea jellyfish use tentacles to catch prey.

5 The submersible glides through the water.

6 deep-sea anglerfish

mini sub equipped for underwater exploration

The pilot and two others squeeze inside the small cabin.

The mini sub protects the divers from pressure and the cold. Outside the submersible, the weight of the seawater above would crush a human. The water temperature is close to freezing, at 37–39°F (3–4°C).

Deep-sea exploration

The deep ocean is the last truly undiscovered place on Earth. More people have been to the Moon than the deep ocean. About 99 percent of it is still unexplored, and there are many new discoveries still to be made.

Mir is a Russian submersible that has explored the deep-sea regions of the Antarctic and Arctic. Here it is being launched from a ship.

The Mir life-support system can support three people for three days.

Life on the ocean floor is examined from the Mir submersible. Mir can take video footage and photographs and collect specimens with a mechanical arm. It can reach depths of 19,700 feet (6,000 meters).

Ratfish eat the remains of sea creatures that have died and sunk to the ocean floor.

Lantern fish are covered in little spots of light, which may attract prey. They produce it with a chemical reaction like the one that lights up glow sticks.

The dumbo octopus has fins a bit like elephants' ears.

The sea pig is a type of sea cucumber that travels across the deep-sea floor, sucking up tiny particles of food in the mud.

deep-sea anglerfish

The deep-sea anglerfish is just one of 20,000 species of **fish** found in the world's oceans. All types of fish have a backbone, scales, fins, and gills.

Animals

The blue-ringed **octopus** is one of the world's most poisonous animals. Octopuses have large brains for their size and are very intelligent.

The **Moon** is the driving force behind tides. Its gravity pulls at the world's oceans, making them rise and fall as the Moon circles Earth.

An **Aqua-Lung** is a piece of equipment that allows people to breathe underwater. It consists of a high-pressure cylinder of air or a special mix of diving gases.

Science

Whale-watching expeditions allow scientists to keep track of where whales go each year and to learn about individual animals and their behavior. Tourists can often join in, too.

humpback whale

A **rock pool** is a great place to start exploring the oceans. Count different types of seaweed and shells, and see if you can spot crabs, shrimp, fish, and starfish.

People exploring

Beaches need to be kept free of **garbage**, which is a disaster for wildlife. Animals can choke on or get trapped by plastic. Pollution kills animals and plants.

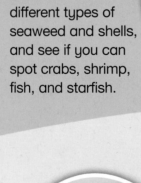

Coral reefs around the world are in danger. Pollution destroys many reef creatures. Warming waters cause corals to lose the algae they need to survive.

Conservation

More to explore

harp seals in the
Arctic Ocean

The **harp seal** is a marine mammal, like whales, dolphins, and walrus. It can stay underwater for a long time, but it comes to the surface to breathe air and also spends time on land.

They may not live in the water, but many kinds of **birds** depend on the oceans for their food. This gannet dives deep into the water to catch fish.

Arctic animals are well adapted to survive the cold. Fish that live in polar seas produce a special antifreeze that stops ice crystals from forming inside their bodies. This keeps the fish from freezing solid.

Arctic cod

Some animals that live in the deepest, darkest parts of the oceans are **bioluminescent**. This means that they glow in the dark. Chemicals in their bodies allow them to do this.

Marine archaeologists study shipwrecks and other evidence of human history in the oceans. They may examine objects on the seabed or carefully bring them to the surface.

A **deep-sea submersible** allows scientists to travel to the farthest depths of the ocean —as deep as 19,700 feet (6,000 meters)! There they can take photographs and collect samples to study.

deep-sea
submersible

Many **dolphins** are protected species, which means that it is against the law to harm them. Even so, many are accidentally hurt by fishing nets.

Global warming is causing the ice sheets at the poles to melt. This makes life even harder for polar animals and will cause sea levels to rise around the world.

Index